I AM INSPIRED TO WRITE THIS story for many reasons. Firstly, my inspiration comes from the many people I have worked with throughout my career as a teacher, counsellor, and social worker. I have learned so much from these people and cherish their stories. My own journey has also inspired me to write this book. I am proud to say that I have accomplished many amazing things, regardless of the adversities I have dealt with along the way. My reliance comes from my faith, my life purpose, and the network of people who believed in me: my late husband, who consistently encouraged me; I carry the values that my mother instilled, including the importance of unconditional love and compassion for impoverished people. My children inspire me daily with their unconditional love support. Lastly, my grandchildren are still young, but their laughter fills my heart. It is amazing to see how their personalities form and how a loving network can really foster resilience in children. I am so thankful to God, whom I call "Babaji." He gave me the strength and courage to write this book and fulfill my dreams.

The girl in the window looks out and sees
The deadened grass but the flourishing trees.
She thought to herself, How could this be?
From nothing came a beautiful tree.
She heard a voice say,
"If majesty can grow from dormant earth,
Then, my child, I give you a rebirth.
Fly from here, escape this pain.
You are royal, now take your reign.
Show the world the majesty that is you."
And with that, the girl grew wings and flew.

–AS–

Introduction

WHEN I GOT MARRIED AT twenty-two years old, I moved away from home. This move was not to the next town or city; this move was across the Indian Ocean. I was suddenly thrust into a life I was completely unprepared for. I was forced to adapt and adjust to the norms and lifestyle of my new family (my partner and my in-laws) and new cultural environment. I did not have a social network to support me, as this was long before we had access to long-distance telephone calls, emails, or social media. I felt alone and scared. This experience led me to my career as a social worker.

The story I am writing is a familiar one, especially for immigrant women. The struggles women face, especially immigrant women when it comes to the relationships between couples, extended family members, friends, neighbors, colleagues, and children, are complex. Much like myself, many of these women are thrown into a new, unfamiliar world.

As a therapist and in my personal life, I have found that many immigrant women struggle with navigating their relationships, while adjusting to their new lives. This book is for those women who are struggling with their relationships, conflicting value systems, and are trying to adapt to their new families and extended families. Above all, this book is for the women who want to learn about the importance of resilience and overcoming their adversities.

This book is divided into eleven chapters, and within each chapter I have woven my life story and my professional story to illustrate a given concept. Although pseudonyms have been used for all the names and locations, the stories are relatable for many. Throughout my years as a therapist, I have found the practical life stories that we share help us to understand our own lives better and to see that we are not as different as we may think. That is why I have chosen this method to discuss the concepts of familial relationships and conflicts, resilience, socialization, values, and beliefs.

In the first chapter, I share the story of my journey, where my personal and professional stories of conflicts and triumph come together. In the second chapter, I discuss the impact of globalization and the intermeshing of cultures as a phenomenon that brings a new dynamic to relationships, including conflicts. The third chapter describes the idea of familial responsibility and the way values, feelings, and behaviours are often learned patterns of learned (positive or negative) behaviour. In the fourth chapter, I outline ideas of resilience, including the importance of a social network. It is impossible to escape from one's shadow, so the best way to confront it is to accept that values inherited are part of one's characteristics. In the fifth chapter, the discussion is based on conflicts in relationships and how to address conflicts from a place of peace.

The sixth chapter involves the ideas that surround ego and the ego trap. I refer to ego as a way to label or identify ourselves. Within this chapter, I discuss how the ego plays a vicious role in relationships and how to bring awareness to the ego trap. In the seventh chapter, I discuss the role of socialization is for the individual and for the couple. I delve into the idea of socialization and how it works throughout one's life and how it is pivotal in our growth, well-being, and progress. The eighth chapter brings to light the complexity of the values and belief systems that we store and how these systems impact our behaviours, particularly in relationships. I have defined *values* as the standards or principles by which we base our lives and make choices, while *beliefs* are assumptions that we hold as being true and real. In the ninth chapter, I discuss the way in which I have practiced gratitude, prayer, and meditation to overcome my personal struggles. The tenth chapter focuses on finding your authentic self, while the last chapter offers a summary of the book through in-depth exercises and the author's reflections for each chapter. It is my hope that my readers will gain new insights into their lives.

Chapter 1

MY JOURNEY

I WAS THE YOUNGEST OF FIVE siblings. My parents were teachers in Lahore, Pakistan, and moved to India in 1947, a month before India and Pakistan gained independence. This was a tumultuous time in history. There were wars, poverty, and overall unrest. When I was just three months old, my family escaped Pakistan and came to India as refugees. My journey, from the start, was one of adversity and resilience.

It took my parents seven years to save for our first home. It had two bedrooms, one of which I shared with my three sisters and my mother. My mother was a hardworking woman. She taught us all how to stay positive and grateful, even amidst hardships. She eventually became one of the first female headmistresses at a local elementary school and started a breakfast program for students who could not afford to eat. As the youngest child, I did not have much, but I never felt like I lacked anything. I was always proud and confident about who I was and where I came from.

At twenty years old, I completed my Bachelor of Education Degree and then had to work in a teaching position in a very small village in the district of Shimla, Himachal Pradesh, India. The village sat seven thousand feet above sea level and was picturesque. At that time in my life, I could not appreciate the beauty of the location because I felt so isolated. The hardest part of this endeavour was having to adjust to a new community with new customs, traditions, beliefs, and taboos. This happened fifty years ago, and I still remember how hard it was.

As I reflect on that period, I believe that I felt different from the other teachers, partly due to the age difference and partly because I felt like a city girl who had been forced to work in the country. As much as I wanted to distinguish myself from the small village and its people, I could not help but be touched by the community, which was generally poor and lacked resources. The students lacked school supplies, warm clothes, and even shoes. The residents were simple and lacked cultural finesse but were respectful and friendly. From this experience, I learned the importance of compassion toward those in need and a sense of gratitude for what I have. After I returned to my city, I furthered my education and completed a master's degree in education.

Soon after I had completed my degree, I was encouraged by my family to meet a suitor, whom I fell in love with after our first supervised meeting. Some may call this an arranged marriage, but I always felt like it was more than that. Although our parents introduced us and we met fewer than a handful of times before we were married, I fell in love!

I was only twenty-two years old when I moved to East Africa with my husband. Life was a challenge, with feelings of joy and loneliness and sadness. I missed my family, particularly my mother, and the comforts of home. I had my first child at twenty-three years old, and my in-laws came to live with us. My relationship with my in-laws and my husband's social network often left me feeling uneasy and uncomfortable. I was very shy and did not know the rules of high-class society, fancy hotels, and clubs. My mother-in-law would often remind me that I was a refugee and did not come from the same class as her family. My in-laws perceived me as an outspoken daughter-in-law with little understanding of how the world operated. I never did learn how to keep quiet the way they wanted me to. In fact, if I felt that my values and my integrity were attacked, I would often reply with a knee-jerk response.

After a few years, we moved to central Africa, and I worked as a schoolteacher. It was a good opportunity for me to meet and socialize with new people, and it was one of our happiest times as a family. I remembered my husband playing poker with friends, and since I did not know how to play, I stayed awake most of the night, caring for our children. The next morning, when I went to work, I looked very tired. Some of my work friends were kind and empathetic and brought tea to help with my fatigue. That simple act was memorable for me, because it was the first time someone had cared for me. I really missed that type of nurturing. It made me miss my own family and a social network.

After fifteen years of living in Africa, we immigrated to Canada. I got my first job in a garment factory. I was sewing gloves and had no idea how to operate a factory-grade machine. A few days into the job, I inquired about a lunch break. The women who worked there, most of whom were immigrants, told me they were meant to eat lunch at their sewing machine station. I was appalled by this and spoke with the supervisor. I advocated for the employees to have a proper lunchroom. I was fired the next day. The management said that my production was below its level of expectation. As I reflect at this moment, I realize that I was always an activist for change, for those affected by injustice, and for female equality.

Being fired from a job that was not utilizing my qualifications as a teacher was discouraging. However, I soon realized this failure was a stepping-stone to propel me forward into my actual career. I decided to upgrade my education and received further training and advancement in working with women, specifically with victims of domestic violence. Eventually I became a social worker with a master's degree. I believe you do not always choose your career, but it chooses you. This was very fitting for my life. My life experiences have given me the lens to look at the adversities and challenges of women through a unique and understanding perspective. For this, I am eternally grateful.

For the last thirty-six years, I have been working as a counselor, social worker, college instructor, and probation officer. I provide therapeutic and educational awareness through group support to men, which gave me the opportunity to understand men as both offenders and victims of violence. My relationships with people throughout my career have been very fulfilling, supportive, and nurturing, but as a social worker, it was challenging to work within my own ethnic community, especially in the area of domestic violence. I was often the subject of people's anger and blame and was even threatened. I was able to persevere through the verbal attacks because I believed I was making a difference in people's lives. I used my knowledge, skills, and other resources to make sure people had access to the social services, language services, and other support systems for themselves and their children.

I volunteered my time to develop projects and programs to support women and immigrant women who were living in domestic violence. At the time, there was less public awareness in the Southeast Asian community about domestic violence and the impact it had on families and children. With the support of professionals, government resources, and ethnic communities, I developed an immigrant women's support and advocacy group that bridged the language and cultural gaps. I soon became recognized, not only in my own community but also within various immigrant communities and social services. At the time of my retirement, I was honoured by the minister of justice for my work in implementing multicultural domestic violence programming.

I felt honoured to be recognized and respected in the immigrant community. I drew strength and happiness from my volunteer work. However, things suddenly took a turn when my husband became ill and had a life-threatening heart attack. I was in my early forties and was forced to leave my outreach volunteer work to pay the accumulating bills. I had three children, ranging from ten to seventeen years old. My husband became very depressed and helpless. He was no longer able to support the family financially, and he was unable to resolve arguments between his parents, who were living with us, and me. This was a very challenging and stressful time in my life. I resented my husband for not advocating for me with his parents and instead leaving the family burden on my shoulders. Inevitably, this had a negative impact on my relationship with him. Things started to deteriorate to the extent that he became so jealous of my recognition in the community that he told one of my close friends that I no longer had time to continue my volunteer work. I was shocked to hear this from my friend. I felt betrayed by my spouse. I identified myself with this volunteer work, and it was so very meaningful for me. However, considering his illness, I understood the reasons why he had said this and accepted his decision.

I soon became isolated from the social groups and community activities that had given me happiness, a sense of purpose, and connection. To keep my family afloat, I kept occupied with multiple paying jobs and did not have any energy or drive to socialize with community groups or friends.

When reflecting on this period, I realize that it was a big shock to my self-identity; I felt I had lost my soul. Many years later, I tried to reconnect with the volunteer groups I had once started, but the connections and relationships had changed.

Chapter 2

THE INFLUENCE OF CULTURE AND FAMILY IN RELATIONSHIPS AND CONFLICT

I N THIS MODERN WORLD OF globalization, cultures are intermingling and influencing each other at a fast rate. This cultural influence also impacts the traditional sense of arranged marriages. In the baby boomer generation, arranged marriages had just begun to be influenced by globalization. My own marriage was one of those. My marriage was arranged by my father, who had placed an advertisement in the matrimonial section of our local city newspaper. My husband's relatives saw the advertisement and notified his family, who were residing in India. One month later, my husband flew from Africa and came to visit me with his family. He then asked to join me for coffee, and my parents escorted us on our "date." We had one or two other meetings before he headed back to Africa. One month after our date, my parents received a telegram giving us one week's notice to arrange the wedding and get married. Initially, my parents did not want me to marry him because he lived abroad, but because I was in love with him, they reluctantly agreed. Even though I chose my partner, it took me a long time to adjust to him and his parents. At the beginning of our relationship, I felt attracted to him, and he felt the same way, but our connection was short-lived. I was isolated from my family and friends, while he was surrounded by his.

This isolation had a negative impact on my relationship. I remember a time when he left me with his family for ten days, as he had to go on a business trip. His family was very cold and made me feel like a stranger. Upon his return, I told him of my feelings. Brushing my feelings aside, he callously said, "It will get better." My relationship with my husband started to deteriorate afterwards. Within five years of marriage, and with two children, we had become strangers.

My relationship with my husband grew more strained as my in-laws were increasingly more involved in our lives. They were living with us, and we were often in disagreements. As the youngest child in my family, I was a free spirit whose feelings were often indulged. My husband, on the other hand, was the eldest son and was looked upon by his siblings as a father figure. When my husband and I had an argument about his family, he would take a neutral stance. I always resented him for not siding with me during a disagreement with his family, but because of how he was raised, he had felt obliged to maintain a responsibility to his parents and siblings. Those years became even more difficult for me because of my negative self-talk about my relationship. I told myself that because my husband did not support me, he did not love me. I felt very alone and unappreciated in my relationship during that time and had no close friends or relatives to lean on. As a result, I built a fortress of anger and resentment around myself and became alienated from my husband and his family members. My in-laws perceived me as shrewd and cold and did not treat me with the warmth and care I so desperately craved. In turn, I fed into their perceptions and continued to build my wall of self-protection. As I look back on this period of my life, I see that my own actions and behaviours needed to change. I should have continued to be my authentic loving self and not crushed my spirit by living in anger and resentment. When we are young and inexperienced and have very little guidance or support, it is difficult to see the error in your ways.

Jesse was a thirty-year-old first-generation immigrant woman whom I had treated in therapy. She came from a traditional family and was forced into an arranged marriage. Jesse was divorced and had immigrated to Ontario with her father and stepmother. During therapy, she disclosed that she witnessed her parents' abusive behaviour toward each other, and she was constantly criticized by her parents. As a result, she was unable to love herself or others. Jesse was very angry and bitter. Although she admitted that she had been equally responsible for her unhappy marriage, accepting responsibility for her own anger and bitterness was challenging. Jesse was fortunate to have a family member (stepmother) to guide and support her. Her stepmother empathized with her past trauma and with love, nurturing, and regular therapy, Jesse overcame her negative behaviour patterns. She eventually remarried, but this time, she was in the mind space to receive and exchange love on a different emotional level.

Family involvement has the potential to improve relationships or destroy them. When we enter an intimate relationship, whether it begins as an arranged marriage or a traditional marriage, the burdens and family baggage that each of us carries has a symbiotic impact. Every relationship will be influenced by our past. The best remedy is to remind ourselves to save the present moment. I emphasize the present because the past is gone and the future is unknown. If you have healthy love, why not bask in it and enjoy the moments that are in front of you, instead of infiltrating them with the past or future. With that said, as a therapist, I have encountered couples who have been living in unhealthy relationships all their lives and feel powerless to bring about changes. Therefore, the negative impact of an unhealthy relationship not only affects the partnership but also has a lasting impact on their children.

The Unselfishness of Love

Whether a marriage is arranged or not, the involvement of the outside world is almost inevitable. We interact with our families, friends, coworkers, neighbors, etc. As I had mentioned, I was isolated from my family and had to rely on my husband. Although he was a good and kind person, I felt isolated from any sort of social connection.

We made the big move to Canada to be closer to my husband's family. Unfortunately, due to a lack of opportunities to pursue a career in his own field of work, my husband began to feel helpless and depressed. Within a couple of years, even more serious health issues surfaced. He had suffered a massive heart attack. For my three children and me, it was a setback that seemed insurmountable at the time. What happened after his heart attack was devastating for our family. Our roles and responsibilities shifted completely, making me the breadwinner, while my husband had to stay home to take care of his health. As our life together took a quick turn, I found myself facing the basic challenges of survival: caring for my children, making sure the financial needs of the family were met, providing care to my husband. I was trying to keep our life from falling apart. I loved my husband, but the idea of romantic love took a back seat for many years.

I vividly remember one day when he asked to meet me for lunch at a coffee shop. He wanted to discuss an engineer assistant position, where he would cover night shifts. I responded with enthusiasm, as the salary was decent, and he would still be home to pick up the children after school. After seeing my enthusiasm, my husband began to cry. He said he was ashamed to work the night shift as an assistant, and it was hard to bring himself to a level that was so beneath where he once was. I looked at him and saw the face of a young boy, fearful and ashamed for the world to see him the way he saw himself. I remember being flooded with empathy for this man I loved so deeply. I told him that if he did not like the hours, he should not take the position. I phrased it in such a way that he did not feel embarrassed about backing out of the job. His face instantly lightened with relief and gratitude; we never discussed that day again. However, I often reflect upon that crossroads. How would my life have changed if I had encouraged him to take the job? I know I made the right choice, because the choice was out of love and an unselfish understanding of what my partner needed.

It's important to understand that women can work with their partners to create a strong familial team, but when those patriarchal family roles are reversed, the societal stigma can affect the whole family. Our family roles had shifted, and we felt the stigma in our community. However, we chose to isolate ourselves, and that feeling of judgment and stigma grew in our own subconscious. I regret not sharing our struggles with my immediate family and my in-laws and friends. I was raised not to discuss private family matters with the outside world. I was taught not to air your dirty laundry and that you did not need to build relationships outside of your family network. Today, I realize that we all must seek a network of friends or family who can provide the emotional support, warmth, and connection that we require. This network allows us to unburden ourselves and release the contempt and stigma that we carry.

Molly and her husband were in their early sixties when they came to me for counseling. Molly's husband was a businessman who invested his time and money into growing his wealth, while neglecting his family's emotional needs. Molly spent years of her marriage trying to convince him to spend more time with her and the children, but he would say he was working hard to provide luxuries for the family. Molly was so disheartened with her life that she decided to separate from her husband after forty years. She could no longer convince him to spend time with her and invest in the relationship. She felt like her life was meaningless and empty, without a connection to her partner. As their therapist, I remember thinking, *What could've been done to avoid the situation that they were facing?* My advice was the same advice I had followed in my own life: support each other's emotional needs unselfishly, with empathy and love. Authentic loving relationships come from the place of purity—where you want to see your partner happy, not by your standards but by theirs.

Blake, a forty-five-year-old man, was receiving group counselling, as part of a men's group. He shared a story about how when he comes home, his three children, wife, and elderly parents used to scatter away from him. Feeling rejected, unloved, and lonely, Blake cried in the group. Robert, another group member, shared that he had experienced a similar coldness from his family, and he was working hard to regain their trust. Robert added that it was not easy, but he was making efforts to change his behaviour. He was trying to look at what they needed from him, instead of what he was providing. Although he was working and earning money, he was not meeting their needs of attention, positivity, and love. When we look at relationships from a position of what our loved ones need and not what we are providing for them, that unselfishness will help to deepen our connections. Relationships are beautiful and inspiring if we can choose to love unselfishly.

Within all of us lives a happy and an unhappy monster. We need to learn to control our negative, demoralizing thoughts and emotions so our family members can enjoy a peaceful, loving, safe, and caring environment. But if the ego takes over and we start using negativity, intimidation, or force, our family unit can be destabilized or destroyed by fear, lack of trust, or even hatred. We must decide, at a conscious level of awareness, to live in harmony.

I recommend reading further about unselfish love in the book *Defending Traditional Marriage* by William E. Harley (2005). Harley is a marital therapist who discusses the ways in which couples can provide an unselfish form of love, which he refers to as "extraordinary care." He discusses the importance of fulfilling your partner's emotional needs through affection, admiration, conversation, domestic support, family commitment, financial support, honesty, and openness.

If we show respect, care, and compassion towards our spouse and family members, we bring positivity into the family. No one can foresee which relationships will endure, the arranged or non arranged. Regardless of how the relationship started, it can only survive and thrive in the presence of trust, honesty, love, respect, friendship, moments of joy, compassion, and dependability.

The exercise below is meant to enhance you own awareness and understanding of your relationship. Try doing the exercises individually and then discussing them with your partner. Ask each other to probe questions, as to why they feel that way and the story behind their viewpoints.

Exercise

1. What does a healthy relationship mean to you? Who would you include in your relationships?

2. How would you rate the importance of the people in your life?

3. Do you think relationships are crucial for happiness, health, success, and social acceptability?

4. How has your culture influenced the way you perceive your relationships – spousal, children, parents, siblings, friends?

5. What qualities would you like to see in your relationships, such as love, trust, empathy, nurturing?

Chapter 3

IDEAS OF RESPONSIBILITY AND COMMITMENT WITHIN A FAMILY

F OR THE PURPOSE OF THIS book, I would like to deconstruct the idea of responsibility. In the *Oxford English Dictionary,* "responsibility" refers to having an obligation to do something or having control or care for someone as part of one's job or role. This definition stresses that the completion of a job or task is managed or controlled by a specific person (the one who is responsible). This idea applies well to the corporate world. In a relationship, responsibility is also important. At home, we are responsible for maintaining safety, care, happiness, love, and integrity in our relationships. We all have a collective role to play. Many of us can apply discipline and work ethic to our jobs, but our attitudes or behaviours in our relationships do not receive nearly the same attention.

Parents usually start giving their children small tasks to help them learn about responsibilities at a young age, and rewards are given for their work. Parents create rules and set boundaries to bring harmony, and children learn about responsibility and accountability by completing these tasks. Children learn best when they are given positive reinforcement, whether it be through verbal praise or tangible reinforcement (candy, small toys, allowance). Children are like sponges; they learn from their parents negative and positive behaviours and the value system.

I saw Mr. Brook for counselling. His wife and child disclosed that he used physical punishment to discipline his son. Mr. Brook was a well-respected member of the community. When asked about his use of discipline, he described his own childhood, where his father would beat him in order to teach him right from wrong. Mr. Brook described his own intentions for physically abusing his son by saying he was protecting his child from bullying and teaching him respect. He described his own childhood as being riddled with bullying. In fact, he was so fearful that his children would be bullied, he prevented them from playing sports or any other extracurricular activities. Initially, I was shocked that someone could justify his abusive behaviour under the guise of protection. In his mind, he was saving his son from the kind of experience that he'd been through, getting bullied and hit by others.

To the outside world, Mr. Brook was a compassionate and respected man, and at home he felt entitled to treat his family with disrespect and abuse. Through counselling, he realized he was not protecting or providing a safe and nurturing environment for his children, and that is why his elder son resented him. Although he was a respected community member, in his own house he did not fulfill his responsibility of being a loving and nurturing partner and father and in turn created an unsafe and negative climate for his family.

Often people in power make the wrong decision in the name of responsibility, protection, and authority. When we identify with our egoistic selves, we lose the gauge between right and wrong. Patterns of behaviour can be challenged by bringing awareness to our negative behaviours and using a cognitive behavioural therapy approach to reframe our thoughts and actions.

The concept of responsibility needs to be emphasized. We are equally, if not more, responsible to our family than to our boss or our job. In the workforce, we generally succeed when we understand our goals and set objectives to attain those goals. This is part of our job responsibilities. If we do not complete this, we will not get paid or even worse, lose the job.

If we extend this concept to our home life, then we must ask ourselves, what is our goal in our family, and what objectives are we implementing to achieve the goal? For most families, the goal is to create and maintain a peaceful, nurturing, and happy environment. This is our responsibility to ourselves, our partners, and our children. Therefore, by applying the same rules of setting goals and objectives and monitoring our progress, we are setting our families up for success. Different family members may carry different responsibilities to improve the climate of the home. With that said, the age, abilities, and health of each family member must be considered. The goals and objectives need to be doable and not daunting. For example, for one family member, an objective may include the way in which he or she talks to his or her partner and children, ensuring the message is delivered respectfully and kindly. A comparison of the office and the home world provides us an understanding of the leadership qualities that we need to create a harmonious, trusting, and respectful environment.

Mr. Simon was receiving counselling as part of a men's anger and conflict-resolution group. In the session, he declared that he was a caring and responsible husband and justified this by saying he gave his wife a ride to work every day. He added that his wife was the one who was ungrateful because she was causing him to be late. After I had an individual session with his wife, she revealed that although they had a second car, Mr. Simon refused to let her drive it.

Contrary to his claims of being caring and responsible, Mr. Simon was using his authority to control his wife. When this matter was discussed in the group, he felt ashamed of his controlling behaviour. Mr. Simon was using his role as responsible provider to control and abuse his wife.

When one partner has witnessed either abusive or controlling behaviour patterns while growing up, he or she often uses the same power and control techniques to intimidate his or her spouse and children and uses manipulative thought patterns to justify negative actions.

In order to move away from these abusive and controlling patterns, we must bring awareness to our actions and then learn the positive ways to interact with our family and with ourselves. These changes do not occur overnight; it is a long process of awareness, learning, and healing.

Tai was a client I saw regularly for therapy for six months. Tai was a firm believer in traditional family values. He believed the man is the head of the family and the wife stays at home and takes care of the children. Because of his patriarchal viewpoints, he was unhappy to have me as his counsellor. He felt that as a woman, I was incapable of counselling or teaching him.

As his therapist, my responsibility was to help him develop a strategic plan that addressed the expected goals. I developed a therapy plan that included his short-term and long-term goals, information, delivery strategy, rules, and expectations. For the first three months, Tai hardly spoke during our hour-long sessions but would leave with some handouts or written material. As the months went by, he gradually became more comfortable and started sharing his thoughts and feelings. It was inspiring to see how he started to change his patriarchal beliefs regarding women and counselling. After six months, things had remarkably shifted for Tai. He thanked me and wrote a heartfelt card expressing his gratitude.

No matter how strong our belief system is, or how committed we are to negative ideologies, we can change. Tai was sixty-five years old. He had spent sixty-five years submerged in an environment where women were considered beneath him and men were the heads of the home. This type of change requires awareness, commitment, and the motivation change. Tai was now understanding that his responsibility was not to be the head of the home but instead to cocreate a happy, loving, and nurturing home.

My work as a probation officer and counsellor was some of the most inspiring times of my life. I felt that my life purpose was being fulfilled. I thoroughly enjoyed delivering domestic violence educational programs to meet the needs of ethnic minority groups. It takes commitment, dedication, and support to see and reap the benefits of change.

Exercise

1. Who do you identify with in the above picture and why?

2. What is the current climate in your family?

3. List 5 of your responsibilities to create a positive familial climate.

Chapter 4

TAPPING INTO YOUR STRENGTH AND RESILIENCE

I N THIS CHAPTER, I HAVE chosen to discuss the importance of a support system and resilience. Having a network of support provides us with a sense of hope and freedom, where we are not afraid to fail. If we do, we trust there will be someone there to help pick us back up again. This type of freedom allows us to move past our adversity and continue our journey without the fear of failure. As I watch my daughter teach my granddaughter how to read, she continually sends a message of encouragement. Although my granddaughter sees reading as a challenge, her mother is continuously encouraging her, regardless of her mistakes. In an ideal situation, parents are the support system that allows children to fail and succeed through love and encouragement. This allows the child to express resilience. As adults, we need to seek out a support system that allows us this same sense of freedom.

The values and beliefs we have acquired from our individual experiences are different and unique from our partner's. No matter how successful or independent we become, we cannot escape the positive and negative imprints from our family of origin. You can never escape your shadow; your best bet is to confront it and own the values you have inherited and learn from the negative experiences.

As the youngest child in my family, my actions were often indulged, and my mistakes were overlooked. My parents loved me, and I am very grateful for their care, but I was never taught the art of resilience. I never learned that things may not always go my way and that hardships are inevitable, but the way in which you deal with them is your true success. In my own life, I have seen hardships, but I have learned that resilience does not mean facing your problems alone and independently. It means accessing the love and support that surrounds you. Tapping into that source of love and connection allows resilience to be possible. A few years ago, my daughter became very ill. At the time, she had a three-year-old daughter and was basically bedridden for one month. She had to take a leave of absence from her work. Watching her triumph and heal herself taught me even more about resilience. I was there for her, along with her spouse and siblings, as sources of love, support, and connection. She used her support system and her motivation to improve and utilize acts of resilience. Tapping into a source of love allows us to gain the strength to conquer adversity.

When coming to a new country, it is not easy to build a social network. Traditional families generally have strong bonds and loyalty among members. There is some difference in the way traditional families think about their relationships and perceive their autonomy. One significant difference involves the way the traditional family is geared around self-sacrifice for the benefit of the family. This often falls upon the matriarch. This was the case in my own life. I sacrificed my social life, my fitness, and often my health, in order to ensure my family was taken care of. In many cases, the modern family is different. They do not want outside involvement in their personal lives, and often they are more willing to voice their needs for self-care. I have worked with many traditional families, and when there is a lack of empathy and instead more of a sacrificial demand with issues of power and control, the ideal traditional family can suddenly become an abusive relationship. Often, the immigrant family relies on each other for emotional needs, but from my personal and professional experiences, I really emphasize the importance of a social network. When adversity strikes, the social network can often be the net that helps catch you.

I worked with a client named Sita, who was emotionally abused by her husband. Sita was participating in a women's support group with twelve other women. Her family was going through some hardships in adjusting to Canadian life and culture. Her husband was an electrician in his home country, and in order to work in his trade, he had to take additional courses. They did not have any family support or close friends living in Canada and were quite isolated. With the help of the women's group, Sita became motivated to find a job at a grocery store and was encouraged by the group to take care of her own well-being, not just her family's. She loved her husband and wanted to stay in the relationship but did not want the emotional abuse to continue. She continued counseling and developed a social network within the group. With counselling and her newly found social network, she was able to return to her family with a new sense of self-respect and self-worth and under different conditions.

Sometimes we assume that our family support system is enough for us to rely on, and then we are taken aback when in times of crisis they are not around. In my professional work and in my own life, I value the importance of creating a varied support network: family members, friends, neighbors, coworkers, etc. I learned the importance of a varied social network from my own life experience. A year after my husband passed away, my daughter took a new job across the country. I was supportive of her decision but was fearful of being on my own. We had lived in our home for twenty years. It was a haven of memories of raising my children and sharing laughter with my spouse. Three months after my daughter had moved, I decided I also needed a change. My inner voice was telling me that I was far from my children and feeling quite isolated.

I was ready to put my house up for sale but needed to renovate the home prior to listing it. Many loving friends were supporting me with the sorting and decluttering. A family friend referred a painter who seemed reasonably priced and was willing to paint the whole house. On the first day, he brought the paint supplies and seemed nice. However, after an hour or so, he began to follow me around the house, putting the green painter's tape along the baseboards. I was starting to feel uneasy and uncomfortable. Then as I turned around, he exposed himself. I was shocked and did not understand what had happened. I ran from my home and went to my neighbor's house. She was also a social worker, and I relayed the incident. I was in shock as to how this could happen to me. I was educated in this area; how could I have been so naïve to trust this man? When I shared this incident with my colleagues, they all showed me their love, care, and compassion.

When I told my family friend (the one who referred this painter to me), she said that "He painted our house, and nothing happened." I felt like her tone and her words were away of victim shaming me, like the incident was my fault or I had made it up. I felt betrayed by this close family friend. A varied social network is important, because sometimes the people who we expect will have our backs may not. If they are our only support system, we will feel vulnerable and deflated. From then on, I relied on my friend support group and my children. It had been a difficult year and a half for me. I lost my husband, my children had moved away from home, and now this incident. I have found a significant pattern in my own life and the lives of many of my clients when overcoming adversity. In order to step into acts of reliance, there were three common factors: a purpose or goal that needs to be achieved, a social network or a support system, and hope and/or belief that things will change. In my life, my goal was to share my personal and professional experiences in a book. True happiness and freedom in life are achieved when a person realizes the purpose of his or her existence and inner potential. Maybe it is someone's purpose for that moment in time, or maybe it is a more existential meaning.

Whatever it is for that person, this is a step in achieving reliance.

For me, writing was my purpose, to share my experiences with readers. My second step toward resilience was my decision to seek counseling. It was a challenging decision, because as a therapist, I felt like I should be able to solve my own mental and emotional needs. But I had to access a varied support system. I had some friends, my children, but I felt I needed more. I was very shy and hesitant at the beginning but grew to enjoy and learn from my time in therapy. My third step toward resilience lies in my belief system. I did not stop praying, meditating, and believing. Sometimes I would wake up sad and alone in the middle of the night and just pray. My prayers were always about gratitude for what I have and what I am hopeful for.

From my personal and professional experiences, I have learned that no matter how much pain or how many setbacks and destructive conditions one faces, never give up hope. Focus on the present, and try to be positive and surround yourself with a positive network. Life is a blessing, and there are many opportunities to keep smiling. I believe in the power of positive energy and healing, and we as human beings have the power to heal.

Exercise

1. What type of family did you grow up in, and what type of family do you have now?

2. Do you think it's possible to seek family support while maintaining your independence?

3. What diverse social networks do you have?

4. What are your strengths, and how do you build upon those?

5. In this moment in time, what is your purpose, or what do you hope to achieve?

Chapter 5

RESOLVING CONFLICTS

CONFLICTS ARE PART OF EVERY relationship—couples, families, friends, neighbors. Conflicts are challenging, and the way we address the situation is demanding, because it causes unrest, mistrust, and unhappiness. Sometimes conflicts bring positive outcomes because the situation can be used as a springboard to get to the bottom of the problem.

Conflicts in relationships can be pervasive. When I was young, my mother told me a story about how extended families used to live together. Inevitably, interpersonal relationships among family members became quite challenging. My mother believed that when arguments become too intense and heated, it is worthwhile to step back from the issue in order to find alternative ways to get to the bottom of the conflict. Sometimes, the root of the conflict does not lie in the present moment but instead stems from the past or future.

Family dynamics can often bring conflicts, especially when different ideologies are brought forth. Sometimes we adapt to such changes with an open heart, but other time it can create further negative outcomes. I recall an incident that seems very insignificant but was incredibly impactful for me. When my children were less than five years old, I had taken raw chicken from the fridge and was getting ready to cook it for my family. My mother-in-law, who was living with us, rushed in and yelled for me to put it back in the fridge, saying there was no need to cook meat today. I did not say anything, but my husband heard what happened and told his mother that I could cook whatever I wanted. I did not understand that on a specific day of the week, my mother-in-law did not want me to cook meat, because of her religious beliefs. This was not explained to me, so I assumed she was just being mean and controlling. The conflicts in relationships can become very challenging when we do not understand the other person's unique upbringing, values, beliefs, or behaviours.

With a lack of understanding, small conflicts can turn into a big, explosive conflict. My career of assisting and counselling clients with familial conflicts has been challenging, because often neither party wants to surrender. Very quickly, little issues are blown out of proportion, and it turns into a much bigger problem in which people often end up hurting each other.

Here are some guidelines to follow when we find ourselves involved in a conflicting relationship.

1. Take the time to respect and understand the perspectives of the other person before passing judgement.

2. Use compassion and patience to understand what your partner is expressing before responding or reacting.

3. Communicate in a calm and controlled manner, without losing control of the volume of your voice, your words (curse words), or your physical behaviour.

Angelo was a counselling client of mine. He received intervention regarding anger management and cognitive behavioural therapy. Angelo was an angry and controlling man who tried to dominate his wife and daughter and thus had a strained relationship with them. He relayed an incident toward the end of our time together about how his daughter, at age fifteen, went to a party and was meant to be home by midnight. Ten minutes before midnight,

Angelo said he was starting to lose control. All the negative thoughts started to flood his mind about his daughter. He imagined his worst fears. Was she drinking? Was she in a car accident? However, he converted his negative thoughts to positive ones and said to himself, *my daughter does not drink or do drugs, and she is going to come home soon, and I need to relax.* His daughter returned home on time, and he was able to greet her with a neutral temperament instead of an anxious, angry, controlling one.

It is easier to repair the conflict before it starts than once we are deeply rooted. Salvador Minuchin (1996), a world-renowned family therapist, described a tool I have often used to resolve conflicts. He described setting up a platform and making a road map to keep focused on the main conflict instead of diverging. Although this type of procedure may seem formal, it guides people in conflict to complete the tasks necessary to address the conflict. When engaged in a conflict, it is key to regroup with a problem summary statement, a purpose, goals, activities, action, outcome, and follow-up. Most minor conflicts have the potential to be resolved, and the cycle of blaming, scapegoating, stonewalling, and hurting each other can end.

If there are contentious issues you and your partner would like to discuss, I have listed some helpful guidelines to resolve the issues without conflict.

1. Prior to discussing, plan a time and place to discuss the conflict.

2. Make a promise to each other to stay positive, calm, and supportive, and allow each other to take a break in order to remain calm.

3. Come up with a strategic plan as to how to address the conflict, and write a list together. It is important to set up a plan and outline a goal and the tasks needed to achieve the goal.

4. Set up a follow-up meeting time, to see if the issue has been resolved.

5. There should be no further discussion about the issue, until the next meeting.

Exercise

For one week, list ten points explaining why you are in a relationship with your spouse.

Examples: I love her/him, I enjoy the conversation and company;

I promised take care of her/him; I am a responsible person

This exercise will help to elicit the vulnerability that is needed to have a trustworthy, nurturing, and supportive relationship.

Chapter 6

THE ROLE OF EGO IN RELATIONSHIPS

THE TERM *EGO* HAS ALWAYS been an elusive term to define. For some, the ego refers to the arrogant self. Throughout my years as a social worker and reading spiritual texts on ego, I have come to define it in my own terms, and for the purpose of this book, as the way in which one prescribes a label to oneself. It is the way we identify ourselves. The ways in which ego drives our relationships and controls our thoughts, emotions, and behaviours can create a division. The ego creates a division, which is based on the idea that we are separate from other people. This is what the ego thrives on, an idea of difference and at times superiority.

For example, our ego in a relationship peaks when we do not accept responsibility for our mistakes and instead blame the other for the mistake. By blaming others for our own mistakes, we identify ourselves as perfect and our counterpart as flawed. Often in relationships, the ego manifests itself when we use "I" statements to create a division. For example, many couples I have worked with will often air their complaints by telling me "I earn more money," "I am smarter at finances," etc. These I statements are meant to create a division of superiority between the two partners. I statements separate us from our love relationships, as they create a division of good versus bad, thereby justifying our negative behaviours. This dance between ourselves, our partners, and our egos can never be fluid.

In my experience, some clients have avoided conflicts by suppressing their emotions and feelings. Although their ego is not voiced, it does not mean it does not exist. The negative and egoistic self-talk still exists, even if it is not voiced. For many of these people, the suppression of these feelings and emotions results in an eruptive behaviour pattern. The way to manage or control these self-destructive patterns involves the release of ego and changing the idea of difference between ourselves and our partner. These changes can be made with conscious awareness, regular practice, and positive self-talk. For example, when a negative thought comes to mind, it needs to stop and be replaced with a positive one. The negative self-talk creates the separation from your partner and allows for the justification of the negative behaviour. As an example, the negative thinking may sound like this: "I am a good person; I work hard, and I am a good provider, but she instigates my behaviour by being so frivolous with money. She doesn't care how hard I work." I statements are used to create a division and inflate our ego and in turn justify our outburst with our partner.

Some people like to live in the past or the future because that is where their ego mind is the strongest. They may identify as a victim in their past or have unrealistic dreams in the future. Unfortunately, the past and future are illusions, and they are simply another way we label ourselves to justify who we are in the present.

Sam and Jenna came for counselling. They were married for seven years and had a four-year-old son. They were embarrassed to share their issues because in their minds, they were the perfect couple. During the process of therapy, I found that they both were very unhappy, as each one was focusing on finding faults in the other, to escape from reality. Both of their minds had been running a marathon of negative feelings of blame, hatred, anger, lack of love and attention on an individual basis. This was a very difficult case, as neither of them was ready to accept responsibility in an open and honest manner and suppress the ego. The goal of therapy was to increase their understanding that ego was the basis of their problems and was hiding under the illusion of "perfection."

They were given a plan to make a list of goals that they wanted their partner to help them with. One of Jenna's goals was to have Sam exercise with her so she could lose some weight. Within the first three weeks, Sam helped his wife with her exercise program. Sam's wish was to have fun and go out and live a more carefree lifestyle, like they had done before they had children. Jenna arranged for a babysitter to come over twice a week for a few hours, so she and Sam could do some of the activities they did prior to having children. By addressing the illusion of perfectionism, both partners were able to set aside their need for ego and superiority and instead work together on specific goals. The couple learned to lean on one another to achieve their goals, and they soon began having a fun-loving and happy life together. We get trapped with the ego when we let our past upbringings, life circumstances, future burdens, and perceptions of society influence and infiltrate our present moments.

The illusion of the ego makes us believe we are our own identity labels. These labels can be prescribed by parents, teachers, or even ourselves. However, this is not our authentic self. Our authentic self is pure and loving, forgiving and altruistic. By living in the present, we can erase the labels that were once imposed. As a level 2 Reiki student, I was taught five ideals: Just for today, I will let go of my anger; just for today, I will let go of my worry; just for today, I will give thanks for many blessings; just for today, I will do my work honestly; just for today, I will be kind to my neighbor and every living thing. These ideals were helpful reminders of staying in the present, as they remind us that all we have is today, is this moment.

Maya was a client who was attending a women's support group because her husband was abusive. Maya had an arranged marriage in India. Her husband had immigrated to Alberta, Canada, and told her family he was an engineer. Maya had just completed her teaching degree in India. When she came to Canada with her new husband, she was surprised that he was not an engineer but instead worked at a gas station. She felt like he had lied to her family and she was trapped. He was a heavy drinker and did not respect her. He belittled her looks and forced her to have cosmetic surgery on her nose and face. He then made her live in the basement until her face healed. After two weeks, she climbed out of the basement window to the police station to get help. The matter was reported, but he denied all the allegations and then put pressure on her to return home. It was a very sad experience, but Maya did not go home until her husband completed his two years of probation. After his probation period, he stopped drinking and attended Alcoholics Anonymous. Maya's husband's ego led him to believe that he was superior, and thus he abused her emotionally and psychologically. Initially, he denied having an addiction, but he eventually surrendered his negative behaviours and accepted his responsibility and went on a healing journey. It is not easy to acknowledge one's weaknesses or shortcomings because of egocentric behaviours that take control over our emotions and feelings.

Mr. Willow, a client whom I counselled, felt trapped by his past life and found it impossible to live in the present after surviving a major heart attack. Mr. Willow came to Canada from Uganda. He had been well settled in Uganda and was a recognized chemist. He boasted about his house, his money, and his children, who were going to a private school. After coming to Canada, he found that life was very hard. He was unable to find a job in his profession, and he had difficulty adjusting to the culture and lack of social status. His self-worth took a turn, and he continually tried to live in the future, dreaming of becoming a millionaire and escaping from his responsibilities of being a father. Unfortunately, he lost most of his money in the stock market and gambling, and his dream of becoming rich was shattered. Mr. Willow lost his confidence, happiness, and health because he could not accept where he was in the present. The illusory ego convinced him that money would make him worthy, and he was in a constant search for that worthiness. He was lucky to have a loving family to support him, and eventually he did learn to love and accept his worthiness in the present, or else his life would continue to be destroyed.

The above stories demonstrate how attachment to the past or future fuels our negative thought patterns and behaviours. The only true escape is to live in the present. Sometimes it is hard to change because of our own belief system and values. However, these beliefs and values also feed the ego trap and make it hard to think beyond our set ideals.

Exercise

1. List ten ways and examples of how you identify yourself.

2. List ten ways and examples of how you identify your partner.

3. Compare the two lists. Can you find similarities between your list and your partner's?

4. Give examples of five identity labels that you and your partner share.

Chapter 7

THE PROCESS OF SOCIALIZATION ON AN INDIVIDUAL AND COMMUNAL LEVEL

SOCIALIZATION IS A PROCESS THAT provides us with an opportunity to understand our values and belief systems in relationship to others. The social context starts from home when an infant is born. The child develops language and understands family rules, morals, responsibilities, customs, values, and beliefs. The socialization process continues for children through their participation in daycare, schools, and activities, and through their interactions with other people (teachers, babysitters, neighbors). Therefore, it is a multilayered system.

In my experience as a therapist, the steps taken toward socialization depend very much on the environment in which we are raised. This includes parents, grandparents, siblings, extended family members, friends, neighbours, academic institutions, places of worship, sports, clubs, workplaces, hospitals, and restaurants. Unfortunately—or fortunately—our values and beliefs do not remain static. They are ever-changing. As societal rules or norms change, our behaviour also changes.

For example, in 1970, I was exposed to segregation when my late husband and two of our close friends travelled to Zimbabwe from Zambia by car. Bulawayo was a big city in Zimbabwe, and it had been a British colony until 1965. Zimbabwe was a landlocked country located in southern Africa. We were a group of six adults and my baby, taking what we thought was a leisurely vacation. Naively, we did not realize the political underpinnings and the ramifications for visible minorities in the country. We did not think of making reservations in a hotel, as we anticipated we would find a place along the way; we were young and free, looking for adventure. The distance from Ndola, Zambia to Bulawayo, Zimbabwe was 1,119 kilometers, and it took almost fourteen hours to reach there. After travelling for some hours, we stopped to get milk for the baby and decided to look for a hotel as well. To our surprise, we were refused. Later, we found out that we were denied accommodations because we were not white. There was a "color bar" where people were segregated based on ethnicity and skin color. We, as a group, were not allowed to stay in a hotel; we had no choice but to stay in a campsite and sleep in our cars. We came from our home countries, where we were accepted and respected. We were shocked and hurt to be treated with such disdain. We continued with our journey and had a good experience in Zimbabwe, which was home to a more bustling city. During our shopping venture, we met a Gujrati man who owned lots of jewelry shops. We told him about our misfortune, and he took us to his home. His family treated us warmly and invited us to stay with them overnight. We were discouraged to travel further and cancelled going to Johannesburg, instead travelling back home the next day. As a result of this experience, the way I interacted within the country changed. I was cautious, reserved, and hurt. This experience in part fueled my emigration from the country.

Socializing as a Couple

With globalization and changes in economic growth, society has become diversified. People in the workplace may be sharing a cubicle, even though they grew up across the world from each other. They may come from completely different ethnicity, religion, culture, and family values. I was always taught that it was taboo for people to marry outside of their ethnicity. I challenge this belief system, because in my experience, limiting a partnership to ethnicity is not a possibility. Relationships are more likely to succeed when we are open to understanding the values and beliefs carried by our partners, instead of holding on to our own societal norms.

Relationships are ongoing acts of socialization. Through every discussion, argument, and behaviour, we bring our values and beliefs. When we socialize with other people outside of our relationship, we allow ourselves to be open to new perspectives, values, and belief systems. For example, an interracial couple I treated for a few months were uncovering the importance of socialization. This couple was often having arguments about child rearing and their expectations of each other. The couple felt that because they were raised in different cultures, their values and beliefs would always be incompatible. I encouraged them to socialize with other couples who seemed to be flourishing. They took my advice and went out a few times with another couple. Through their discussions with their friends, they found that many of their values and beliefs did not align, but they had learned to appreciate those differences or at the very least understand where the beliefs and values came from, in order initiate empathy for their partner. For the same reason, it is also healthy in a relationship to socialize with personal friends on an individual level. However, we must be cautious of whom we choose to socialize with and what they offer to us as individuals and how they influence our relationship with our partner.

I worked with a couple who were on the brink of divorce. Daby had a wealthy friend whom she had known since high school. Daby enjoyed his friendship and began to envy his luxurious lifestyle. This friendship brought continuous conflict to her relationship with her husband because she compared her middle-class life to her friend's lavish one. Daby's husband had a decent job with a good salary, and she had a secretarial job. They had two children, and in a therapy session, she told her husband that she could not live on his monthly paycheck. Her husband got very distressed with her selfish behaviour. After several therapy sessions, she realized that by socializing with her high school friend, she was destroying her relationship.

In a partnership, it is our responsibility to socialize with people who help and support us and leave us with positivity. In my experience, the proverb "you are the company you keep" is very fitting. As a social worker, I regularly worked with multiethnic men and facilitated men's groups to educate them about domestic violence, anger, and conflict resolution. The members were encouraged to role play what it would look like to change their unhealthy styles of communication. For example, some group members would address their partner as "old lady," and some would address their partner as "Mai" (meaning *servant*). They both are derogatory and degrading terms. When the group members acted out their negative behaviour patterns in front of their peers, they were caught off guard to see how inappropriate and disrespectful their acts of communication were. It was a very powerful exercise, where one's communication style and socializing patterns come to light. Awareness is often the gateway to change.

From my personal experience, I neglected to establish a social network of friends. I now wish I had created time to foster my friendship and receive support when I needed it. When I was young, life was always busy. I was raising my children while working two jobs and volunteering. I did not realize the value of friendships. As women and mothers, we are often admired for being sacrificial for our families, but this societal construct can be detrimental to our mental well-being and can create further isolation. My own mother didn't model the importance of friendships and in fact instilled the value that it was disrespectful to your family to discuss your problems with outsiders. However, this value can enhance isolation and limit you from the joy that friendships harbour.

Socializing from a Familial and Cultural Stance

Positive and negative socialization start at a young age. My granddaughter's first experience at school was initially quite negative. Some of her peers were unkind and excluded her from activities. These peers who exhibited this type of negative behaviour were also learning about how to socialize from their families of origin. Acts of bullying stem from many sources, but the way in which we model our family values and beliefs and show care in our relationships is a contributing factor. As parents, we are responsible to teach our children to respect themselves and other living beings and recognize positive relationships.

As I mentioned in previous chapters, because of globalization, diverse ethnic and cultural groups, and interconnecting, it is crucial to enhance our knowledge and skills about understanding each other's cultural norms and communication patterns. For example, when socializing with women from Southeast Asian cultures, making eye contact, handshakes, hugs, and kisses are inappropriate and can be considered disrespectful. Different groups have a cultural proximity boundary, and we need to understand and respect their circle of personal space.

I recall an experience when I was delivering cross-cultural groups. A co-presenter, Ms. Lam, was discussing cross-cultural communication with the group, and one of the male participants, Fernando, approached her for some clarification. He came very close to her, and she felt very uncomfortable. She tried to back away, and he continued moving towards her until she was literally against the wall. What happened here was very interesting. The participant was invading Ms. Lam's cultural proximity boundary. He did not understand that infringing upon her personal space made her feel unsafe, disrespected, and uncomfortable, because this idea of cultural proximity was different in his home country.

To summarize this chapter, I must emphasize that socialization involves our upbringing, culture, race, nationality, economics, and politics. Although we live in the same society, these factors intersect and can pose a challenge in the way we socialize. Therefore, we must be aware of understanding our differences and each other's value and belief systems.

Exercise

1. List five of your beliefs on socialization. Where do these beliefs stem from?

2. Prioritize these beliefs in your own life.

3. Where does your partner rank in your socialization priorities?

4. List five people you regularly socialize with. With each person, ask yourself if they bring positivity to you and your family life. Do they have a belief system that you agree with; is it a reciprocal relationship?

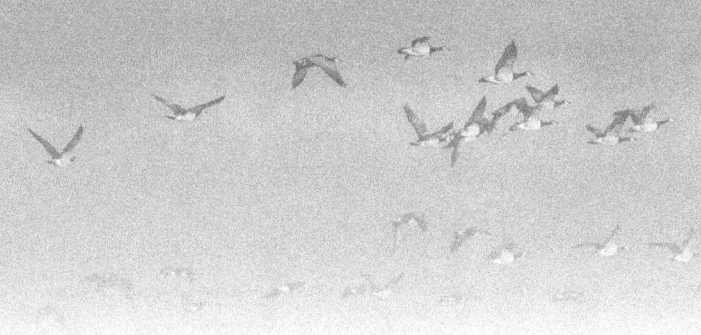

Chapter 8

THE CONNECTION AMONGST VALUES, BELIEFS, AND RELATIONSHIPS

I REFER TO VALUES AS RULES or perceptions set by the family, religious groups, society, and the community, in order to set expectations and boundaries regarding behaviour. These boundaries and expectations are then carried with us and are often used to identify and label who we are. On the other hand, beliefs are assumptions we believe to be truthful. Beliefs emerge from our experiences and then live through our values. To illustrate this concept, it is important to understand the ways in which a child's behaviour is shaped in a family. The influence of a family structure, which is its own microcosm, carries its own restricted rules, boundaries, and assumptions, which contribute to lifelong influence. For example, a mother was charged with child abuse, and her justification was that her parent disciplined her in the same way when she was caught stealing money. Therefore, we justify our behaviour based on our values and beliefs, which are interconnected.

Barbara, a client I was seeing, had come to Canada after marriage. She belonged to a traditional family who emphasized altruistic behaviour and respect for elders in the family. Barbara carried her values from her family of origin and therefore respected her mother-in-law as her own mom. Unfortunately, she was mistreated by her mother-in-law, who told her that she was not her mother. Unfortunately, she felt betrayed by her mother-in-law and angry towards her family for instilling these values.

My personal values and experiences continue to change as my experiences change. My value to help people in need was given to me by my mother. However, my experiences in my career exposed me to acts of racism and sexism. My attitude towards life became somewhat jaded, and although certain beliefs were passed on to me, my life taught me that I needed to be somewhat guarded in opening myself up.

My late husband grew up with a value that success, social status, and family honor were the most important priorities. When he left Africa, he felt like he left behind the status and success and continued to live the latter part of his life in the shadows of hurt and remorse. If my husband was able to release these entrenched beliefs from his family of origin and live in the present, he would have lived a much happier and more fulfilled life. We all have positive and negative thoughts and experiences, and it is within our power to change.

Two years, after moving to Canada from Africa, I received an opportunity to participate in a counselling training program. This was a life-changing experience that changed my attitude and belief system. I participated in a training program along with several diverse ethnic groups: Chinese, Portuguese, Polish, Latino, Laotian, and South Asian. The focus of the training was to prepare participants to help their ethnic communities and become cultural consultants for government and nongovernment agencies. The main goal was to assist new immigrants and refugees in their resettlement process. Most of the participants in the training program had a professional occupation in their home countries such as lawyers, doctors, teachers, journalists, community activists, and engineers.

For two years, all the participants learned from different instructors about human behaviour, networking, community development regarding similarities and differences of values, beliefs, behaviours, attitudes, cross-cultural components, communication styles, translation, and interpretation. The training had two components;

the first year was theory, and the second year was field placement. During the leadership training module, my role was to teach a class of twenty adult students for a few hours and write my observations and comments in a journal. The students were given tasks to complete. There was mistrust among some of the group members about authority and leadership, as they might have been subjected to persecution in their home countries. They exercised their power and lack of respect for me by snatching my observation book from my hand. It was a devastating experience for me as well as for rest of the students. The students' reactions to situations was a result of their fear and lack of trust in the system stemming from their past experiences and beliefs. It was interesting to witness that under stressful circumstances, people could easily switch to patterns of old behaviours.

The same principles apply when we find ourselves trapped in relationship turmoil, where people have different values and beliefs and compromising becomes impossible. For example, I worked with a South Asian grandmother, who while baby-sitting her grandchild used a massage oil to massage the baby, but her daughter-in-law had warned her that the child had an allergy to that oil. The mother-in-law did not agree with her daughter-in-law, and felt she knew better because of her own beliefs. The mother-in-law had low self-esteem because of her past life experiences, when she was treated like an incompetent mother by her husband and his family. Furthermore, the experience triggered her negative self-talk, which was "I am not worthy; I will not be told what to do anymore." Therefore, she went against her daughter-in-law's rules and created friction in their relationship. This example demonstrates how past experiences and negative thoughts, feelings, emotions, and beliefs are stored in our minds and give birth to conflicts and misunderstandings.

Ideas of racism and discrimination often stem from these values and beliefs that have been replicated and integrated into the family culture for generations. For example, I recall a friend of my son's coming to our home and regularly commenting on how it smelled like curry. My son was so embarrassed that eventually he stopped inviting that friend over. This was thirty years ago. Today, my granddaughter's friends come over, and I feed them curry, and they love it. Their parents ask for my recipe. This change is not solely reliant on time but the values and beliefs that children are exposed to and their experiences. This ideology continues in the workplace as well. To change the discriminatory attitudes of others requires intensive training, education, and exposure to positive cultural experiences.

As a social worker, the ethical nature of my job carries its own responsibility. However, I also carry my own values and beliefs as an immigrant wife and mother. I was working with a South Asian woman whose husband threw her down the stairs and damaged her eardrum. She came to see me for therapy. It was my ethical responsibility to report the incident through the proper channels. However, as a mother and a member of the same ethnic community, part of me knew the community would blame me for breaking up a family. I knew I had done the right thing by reporting this man, but it does not remove the values and belief systems that we are exposed to. Sometimes our new belief system still grapples with the external belief system.

As I mentioned in the previous chapters, each member of a partnership comes with their own sets of values and beliefs. Although my husband and I were married for thirty-six years, we were raised with a different set of expectations, assumptions, and values. As a result, our thoughts and behaviours did not match. However, we did share common values, including *honesty, commitment, loyalty, generosity, education, sacrifice, devotion, friendship, meditation/prayers,* and *children.* My husband's negative belief system included *I am the best, I am the decision-maker, I am the powerful man.* My negative belief system included *I am more successful, I work harder than you, I am right.*

In order to manage our differences, I learned to see positivity in our common values and give gratitude to each situation. It is not easy to surrender our egotistical thoughts of being the best, independent, and self-supporting person. Lastly, I tried to communicate to my partner using the voice of *love, commitment, trust, friendship, fun,* and *security.*

When I was growing up, being humble was an intrinsic family value and was often emphasized in my culture. I recall applying for a leadership position and being interviewed by a panel of three executives. I was asked to discuss my achievements, and I felt very uncomfortable, as this was against my modest and humble belief system. When I did not get the position and inquired why, I was told that I did not present my achievements and qualifications with enough confidence. That was an eye-opening experience for me. I learned that the inherited values and beliefs that I coveted do not always serve to your benefit.

Exercise

1. List five common values that you and your partner share.

2. Discuss these values with your partner, and provide examples of how both of you exhibit these in your family.

3. List five negative values and beliefs you carry. Write down where you learned these values and beliefs. Now, beside each negative value and belief, provide a positive counter and how you will incorporate that into your life.

Chapter 9

LIVING WITH GRACE

THE DIVINE, UNIVERSAL ENERGY OR Creator can mean many things to different people. I believe in God. I was raised to believe in one God, whom I refer to as Babaji (which translates to *respected elder*), but I respect and honor the way in which people choose to pray, believe, and express their faith. I believe we are here to serve humanity, to work hard, to pray or meditate for peace, and to help those in need. This is what living a graceful life means to me. In my eyes, the Creator (God), lives everywhere—in every human being, in every life force, in the form of energy. All living things have energy nature: plants, trees, animals. Even though I was raised in the Sikh religion, my experiences have exposed me to the principles of Christianity, Buddhism, and Hinduism, and I have incorporated the loving ideal from those religions into my life.

In my experience, I have seen that our destiny is preordained. We do have free will to make our choices, but some things are not in our control, but instead in the hand of destiny. I have seen miracles in my life that can be explained only by faith. My daughter was conceived, even though my fallopian tubes were tied. Not only that, but she was a breech baby delivered naturally, completely unscathed. My daughter was destined to be born, and she has always been and continues to be my best friend. Another miracle was when my late husband had his first heart attack nineteen years ago. I remember him complaining about chest pain, and my older son and I drove him to the hospital. My son was only seventeen years old, and he drove through a winter storm, right through all the red lights. We got my husband to the emergency room, seconds later he collapsed. His heart stopped, and he was given four defibrillator shocks to revive him. His heart miraculously started again. I believe God worked through my son to help his dad survive.

Every child is born and comes with a purpose. I am also grateful to my second child, who sat in the hospital waiting room countless times while his dad was being treated. He would go straight to the hospital after dental school and sometimes stay there overnight, while trying to pass his own exams. His service to his dad and to me was courageous and admirable, and I would not have survived without his support. It was my destiny to have such wonderful children, and every day I wake up with a sense of gratefulness to God.

I have been through many adversities in my life. I came from a refugee family, on the other side of the world. I have lived on three continents and endured racism, sexism, and traumatic betrayals. I have also seen incredible love from my husband and my children, academic and career success, and have been blessed with the opportunity to change people's lives. I have survived my adversities and relished in my victories, because of my faith in God. My faith has been the backbone of my resilience and triumph.

Chapter 10

FINDING YOUR AUTHENTIC SELF

THIS BOOK IS NOT ONLY about relationships with an outside person (like a spouse or family member), it is also about the relationship we have with ourselves. In this book, I have tried to emphasize that we often cannot control the outside world or the circumstances that occur, but we have control over our thoughts and reactions. Finding our authentic self requires diligent practice of being aware of our thoughts, using tools like meditation, self-reflection, journaling, etc. By living in the present moment, we can reduce the burdens of the past and the future.

This book is not only about my own experiences as an immigrant woman, a mother, and a therapist, but also reflects the journeys of my clients. I have used a holistic approach to discuss various concepts that can be used to improve relationships with partners, family, community members, and yourself. In my personal life, I have found that relationships have been the most complex area of my life. I am saddened to admit that even as a therapist, I always paid more attention to the needs of others than to myself and carried other people's negative comments as baggage from place to place. When reflecting on my younger years, I see that I did not have the courage to speak out with assertiveness but instead used anger to mask my emotions. I thought that standing up for myself would create more conflicts for me, not realizing that by not standing up for my needs, I was creating a conflict within myself that would then lead to more conflicts with others.

There will always be moments in our lives when we wish things could have been different, whether it is an action that we did or didn't do or something we said or didn't say. For these moments, my best advice is to release yourself from the burdens of the past. Look at yourself and forgive yourself. I have always been a fan of Oprah, and in the spring of 2019, I was able to attend an evening presentation with her ("A Path Made Clear"). During her talk, she emphasized the power of forgiveness and said, "When you know better, you do better." This simple phrase has the power to allow yourself to forgive.

I wrote this book with the sincere hope that I can help women who have had similar struggles to be able to empower themselves and heal their relationships. I have always wanted to make sure people have access to meaningful resources, and it is my hope that this book will be a resource for those who are struggling.

The common thread that links each chapter is the idea that in order to bring harmony into our relationships, we need to understand our role in conflicts, our understanding of each other's values and beliefs, and create a resource network, so we are able to feed our own spiritual souls. Every relationship, including the one we have with ourselves, requires care and nourishment.

Chapter 11

WORKBOOK EXERCISES

I N THIS SECTION, I WILL review key concepts from each chapter and provide you with more in-depth exercises to help you maximize your understanding and introspection. The concepts I would like to highlight include self-identity, acculturation resiliency, values and beliefs, family conflicts, responsibility, power and control, and the ego trap.

Your Journey: Exercise 1.1

In the first chapter, I take you on a brief journey into my own life. I would like you to report on your own journey, focusing on the key concepts of self-identity and what it means to be your authentic self.

In this exercise, you will reflect upon your journey with your family, friends, and home country. In a journal, complete the following tasks.

- What was your birth city, country, hospital?
- How was your childhood? Do you have any fond memories to share? What are your three fondest memories?
- What brought your family or you to a new country?
- When you departed from your city and landed in a foreign country, what was your first impression?
- Name three things that you miss from your home country/family of origin.

Author's Perspective

It is very important to allow opportunities for people to share their losses of leaving their surroundings and regaining a new beginning. This is a step towards self-understanding, growth, and an awareness of where we are and where we have come from.

Exercise 1.2

The following exercise focuses on creating a safe place in your body so you can connect with yourself through mirror exercises and recognize your strengths. Therapists use mirror work to help clients connect, love, and understand themselves. Louise Hay was a pioneer in this field. I have adapted some of the ideas of mirror work to help you start creating a space of love, acceptance, and connection to yourself.

- Start by looking in the mirror for a couple of minutes. What do you see?
- Look again, focus deep into your eyes, and this time pay more attention to what is going on behind your eyes.
- Who do you look like (mom, dad, siblings, a movie star, or a sad and defeated human being)?
- How do you feel, when looking at yourself in the mirror? Do you feel sorry for the person in the mirror? Do you feel angry at this person? Do you feel happy and loving towards this person? Be honest in checking your feelings, and promise to pay attention to this person in the mirror.
- Talk to the person in the mirror and let him or her know that you accept and love them for the positive and negative feelings.
- While looking in the mirror, hug yourself and stay locked in the position for a couple of minutes.

- Practice this exercise and write your thoughts, feelings, and emotions in a diary and continue this exercise for twenty-one days.

Author's Perspective

This is a very powerful exercise to reconnect with yourself. I have done this exercise, and it has helped me reclaim my space in my body and slowly empower the body. Once you begin to accept yourself, you begin to understand that you are entitled to feel like a person who is loving and deserving of love.

In Chapter 2, I delve into the ideas of the connection between family and culture and the influence this has on our own ideals and behaviours.

Exercise 2.1

In this exercise, I would like you to think about your family of origin. The family is our first platform to learn about love and safety. The intention of this exercise is to raise an awareness of how a family can foster safety, stability, love, and happiness. On the contrary, not having a nurturing and positive home environment can create a barrier, preventing someone from fulfilling his or her responsibilities and duties towards family.

In a journal, respond to the following questions.

- What does an ideal family look like to you?
- What hopes and dreams do you aspire to achieve?
- Do you think your family is proud of you?
- What message you will like to send to your family of origin or birth?

Author's perspective

The family of origin is the first institution that teaches us what to expect in life. We learn rules and responsibilities by observing our parents, grandparents, siblings, and other extended family members. Some of the expectations are hidden in values, beliefs, and morals. Both positive and negative values are inherited, and it all depends on our outlook.

In chapter 3, I discussed ideas of responsibilities and commitment to our families and ourselves.

This exercise takes a closer look into the responsibilities and commitment of each member in the family to create harmony, love, and safety in the home. In contrast, compare the responsibilities you have at work.

- What steps must you take to ensure that you achieve your goals at work?

- What steps must to you take at home to maintain a harmonious and happy environment with your family?
- What styles of communication did you experience in your childhood? How did this style transfer to your own family? For example, would you hit your child as a form of discipline because you witnessed it in your own childhood?
- How do you communicate respect to your family members?
- Do you have entrenched gender role (example: a man is the provider, and a woman is a caregiver)?

Author's perspective

Within our family, we sometimes tend to excuse our negative behaviours because they were learned in our family of origin, and therefore, we are not at fault. However, in the present moment, we must remind ourselves that we are in control of our minds, thoughts, behaviours, and actions, and past patterns that are negative need to be broken, instead of cycling them through our current relationships. This takes conscious awareness and often therapy to fully grasp the impact of the past.

In chapter 4, I emphasize the importance of social supports and resilience. In order to continue building resilience, it is important to acknowledge and appreciate the acts of resilience we have already used and how we have succeeded.

Exercise 4.1

Adjustment and adaptation are a lifelong process that continues as we encounter new challenges. The focus of this exercise is to raise our awareness about how we learn to adapt and adjust to a new environment or relationship. It could be the experience of going into a new family, a new city, or a new job.

In a journal, respond to the following questions.

- List at least three challenges you faced when coming to a new country/family/job. What steps did you take to survive, adjust, and/or adapt?
- When reflecting upon your experience, how does it make you feel to think about your survival? List at least five positive adjectives describing your feelings.
- What advice do you have for other people going through a similar struggle?
- What would you do differently if you had to relive the same situation?

Author's perspective

I was quite young when I had to adjust and adapt to a new family, a new country, and a new teaching job. I was sheltered by family of origin and did not learn the basic skills of shopping, making friends, cooking, etc. I reflect on this time and praise myself for my survival techniques. I read recipes, consulted an older colleague about socializing advice, and lastly, I used to write about my experiences in a journal. When I reflect on this period, I see myself as resilient, fearless, positive, hopeful, and persistent.

In chapter 5, I highlighted issues of conflict and conflict resolution. The focus of these exercises is to identify the conflicts that appear in your relationship with partners, family members, friends, colleagues, etc.

Exercise 5.1

- Think about a conflict situation with someone who is important to you.
- Does the conflict ever escalate to shouting or becoming out of control? What does this look like? How does each person react?
- What kind of issues emerge more regularly?
- How long it takes you to reach to a calm state?

- When was the last argument? Who was involved? What initiated the problem? What was the resolution?

Author's perspective

In my personal life, I was quite outspoken and confrontational. At times, this escalated simple issues into a full argument. It is important to understand people's intentions, the reason for creating conflicts, and the other person's perspective. My husband and I had full-on argument over a simple situation of what color of liner to pick for the kitchen pantry drawer. It went from something insignificant to an inventory of all our previous issues. Eventually, we both got tired of arguing and took a break. During that time, I realized the fighting was not about the color of the liner; it was about my partner's health issue, fear of losing control over his family, and many other issues around that. For me, it was also a need to have control and not give up my stance. This example demonstrates the importance of taking a break and reflecting on each other's perspectives, including our own.

Exercise 5.2

Thoughts are a very powerful medium that can motivate you or trap you in conflict. It is important to understand that your thoughts have an impact on your mind and body. The positive thoughts can boost your productivity, confidence, and creativity, and on the other hand, the negative thoughts can deplete your energy. The way we speak to ourselves can help us prevent conflict situations. If we acknowledge our learned negative thoughts, then we can see how this affects our arguments and conflicts.

The following exercises focus on positive and negative self-talk.

- When you are late for your office meeting, what thoughts come to your mind? Write them down. Are these thoughts positive or negative?
- When your boss asks the reason for coming late, how do you feel? Are these thoughts positive or negative?
- When you reach home and find that your husband was late picking up your child from school, how do you react?

Now imagine all these circumstances occurred, but the night before, you had positive interactions with your children and partner. In the morning prior to leaving for work, you and your family shared a happy moment. How would these feelings of positivity that were stored inside of you impact the way you handled the problems of your day?

<u>Author's perspective</u>

It is important to understand that the positive thoughts create positive energy, no matter what the situation is, while the negative thoughts block our minds and our productivity. When we start with a positive mindset, we can handle negative situations in a lighter way.

In chapter 6, I discussed the ego trap and how it can be detrimental to relationships. The ego has a way of making us believe we are different from our partner or significant other. Often, we feel superior or justified in behaving a certain way.

The exercises are related to ego and relationship: 6.1.

- In your journal, list five points that your partner or someone close to you has said that bother them or that you feel you need to change.
- Examine each point and provide an example to verify the point. For example: My partner feels like l am selfish. Sometimes I can behave selfishly, especially when I don't help her cook or clean the house.

- After you provide an example for each point, beside the point ask yourself where you learned this behaviour. Did you learn it from your father, mother, friends etc.?
- Lastly, write down a way to improve on this behaviour. I can show my partner that I am willing to help with the chores on Saturday when I am not working. Discuss this with your partner.

Author's perspective

By acknowledging that we are flawed, we bring awareness to our negative behaviours and thus allow growth and positive change into our relationship. Even in my own relationship, I often had difficulty accepting my negative behaviours. I would justify my reactiveness by saying I was standing up for my rights. had learned this reactiveness as a defense and protective mechanism from my childhood. Instead of reacting, I should have taken a break from the conflict and come back to it. when I was ready to express myself calmly.

Exercise 6.2

It is difficult for the ego to live amongst vulnerability. With your partner, express one goal you would like his or her help in achieving in one month's time. Outline the daily/weekly steps it will take for you to achieve this goal with his or her help. Have your partner do the same for you. This exercise allows you both to express a need in yourself that you require your partner to help fulfill.

Author's perspective

I emphasize the need to eliminate the dependency on the "I" statement in a relationship. The purpose of this exercise is to eliminate the idea that we are better or different than our partner, but instead we rely on each other's strengths to become a stronger unit together. This breaks down the barrier of "I" and instead allows you to use "We." When you both accomplish your goals, celebrate this together as a collective victory, not a "me victory."

In chapter 7, I outline ideas about the process of socialization and its importance for resilience, happiness, and fulfillment.

Exercise 7.1

In your journal, write down the three most important areas of socialization that you participate in, whether it be with your spouse, work colleagues, friends, neighbors, religious group, etc. Within those three categories, write down how fulfilling these relationships are on a scale from one to five. If they are low, write down one way to improve or enhance the social experience. Please see the example below.

Example:

Area of Socialization	Spouse	Friends	Church Group
How fulfilled are you with your experience (1 (not fulfilled)-5 (very fulfilled))			
One thing I can add to make this more fulfilling			

Author's perspective

I moved to three continents in the last fifty years, and in many cases, I was able to adjust to my new surroundings because of the connections I was able to establish. When I was in East Africa, a group of teachers and I formed a group, and we would spend one day a month serving the needy in the community. When I moved to North America, my temple, volunteering, and immigrant community organizations allowed me to pursue my passion with like-minded groups of people. Lastly, my husband and I enjoyed socializing with friends at regular dinner parties. The socialization process gave me a platform to broaden my vision and motivate me to look at the world through a window, not a mirror.

In chapter 8, I discussed the ideas of values and beliefs and how we all come from a different mindset but that it is imperative to take the time to understand our partner's perspective. The following exercises will bring further understanding of how this could be achieved.

Exercise 8.1

In your journal, list a conflicting issue between you and your partner that you feel is based on your opposing value system—for example, child rearing or the role of a woman in the household. After you write down what the conflict is, write down why you feel so strongly about it. Does it come from a value or belief that you carry? Then discuss this with your partner and ask him if he is opposed to your viewpoint because of a conflicting value or belief. Now that you understand the background of where the conflict comes from, does it become easier to compromise or resolve the issue?

What is the conflicting issue?	He thinks we should be freer in letting our child go to bed later and be more flexible.
My values and beliefs	I was raised with a strict bedtime, and as a teacher, I believe children need adequate sleep to thrive at school.
My partner's values and beliefs	He was raised in a very free from rules home and believes that children should be raised with more flexibility.

Compromise	Elicit flexibility on Saturday, when there is no school the next day.

Author's perspective

In my own marriage, my husband and I had conflicts where the root cause was based on values and beliefs. My inexperience prevented me from exploring the reasons for our conflicting values and beliefs. One example was when I wanted to learn how to swim, as my young daughter was taking lessons. My husband refused to allow me to take the lessons because there was a male instructor. I did not want to create further conflict, so I accepted it and never took the lessons. In retrospect, I wish I had done this exercise with him and strategized a compromise where I was able to understand his perspective and he could understand mine.

About the Author

SIMRAN HAS A MASTER OF Social Work Degree and has experience as a counsellor, college lecturer, and probation officer. Although Simran is semiretired, she still provides short-term counselling for trauma victims. Simran emigrated from India to Africa and then to Canada. She is a loving mother to her three children and a caring grandmother to four exceptionally special grandchildren. Simran is an activist and continues to foster growth and awareness among individuals, families, and communities in the area of values, beliefs, traditions, communication patterns, and cultural taboos and conflicts.